WIND ENERGY
Blown Away!

Amy S. Hansen

PowerKiDS press

New York

Powering Our World

For my parents and the time spent on windy lakes

Published in 2010 by The Rosen Publishing Group, Inc.
29 East 21st Street, New York, NY 10010

First Edition

Editor: Amelie von Zumbusch
Book Design: Greg Tucker
Photo Researcher: Jessica Gerweck

Photo Credits: Cover, pp. 5, 7, 9, 11, 22 Shutterstock.com; p. 13 Fred Derwal/Getty Images; p. 15 Sarah Leen/Getty Images; p. 17 © Barrett & MacKay/age fotostock; p. 19 Julie Fisher/Getty Images; p. 21 © Emilio Ereza/age fotostock.

Library of Congress Cataloging-in-Publication Data

Hansen, Amy.
   Wind energy : blown away! / Amy S. Hansen. — 1st ed.
      p. cm. — (Powering our world)
   Includes index.
   ISBN 978-1-4358-9327-6 (library binding) — ISBN 978-1-4358-9742-7 (pbk.) —
ISBN 978-1-4358-9743-4 (6-pack)
   1. Wind power—Juvenile literature. I. Title.
   TJ820.H36 2010
   621.31'2136—dc22
                                                    2009022262

Manufactured in the United States of America

CPSIA Compliance Information: Batch #WW10PK: For Further Information contact Rosen Publishing, New York, New York at 1-800-237-9932

Contents

Wind Energy 4

What Makes the Wind? 6

Catching the Wind 8

Electricity from Wind Turbines 10

Farms That Capture Wind 12

Where Are the Wind Farms? 14

Lighter Winds 16

Problems with the Wind 18

Wind Power for Tomorrow 20

Wind Energy Timeline 22

Glossary 23

Index 24

Web Sites 24

Stand outside and feel the wind blow on your face. That moving air has energy. The wind's energy moves sailboats across lakes and turns wind **turbines** to make electricity. When we catch the wind's energy, we have wind power.

Most of the electricity used in the United States comes from **fossil fuels**. However, we are using the wind more and more. Wind power is a renewable energy **source**. This means that no matter how much we use, we cannot use it up. It is also a nonpolluting energy source. When we capture wind energy, we are not putting smoke or other pollution in the air.

The wind powers sailboats, such as these. People have used sailboats for thousands of years.

What Makes the Wind?

Wind can knock over huge trees or cause a single piece of grass to flutter. Whether it is powerful or gentle, wind is here because of the Sun.

As the Sun's rays reach Earth, they warm up the air. However, the Sun does not warm air evenly. For example, air over land heats up more quickly than air over water does during the day. Pockets of air that are warmer than others cause wind. When air gets warm, it rises. Then, cooler air rushes in to take its place. This movement of air is wind. As long as the Sun shines, there will be wind that we can use to power turbines, windmills, and sailboats.

You cannot see the wind, but it is easy to see its power. Light winds move leaves, while stronger winds bend branches.

Catching the Wind

Long ago, the Nile River was like a highway for ancient Egyptians. After paddling their boats downstream, Egyptians put up sails. The sails caught the wind and pushed the boats upstream. Sails are one of the earliest ways people used the wind.

Windmills are another early invention. Windmill **blades** catch the wind and turn. The turning blades power water **pumps** or turn **millstones**. Millstones **grind** wheat to make flour. Windmills were already in use in China and Persia over 1,000 years ago. Later, the Netherlands became famous for windmills that pumped seawater off land. Early American settlers used windmills, too.

These are some of the 19 windmills built around 1740 to pump water off land at Kinderdijk, in the Netherlands.

Wind turbines are windmills that make electricity. Electricity powers lights, TVs, clothes driers, and many other things. We **generate** electricity by moving magnets around **coils** of wires. A wind turbine's job is to use the energy from the wind to move the magnets.

Wind turbines sit on top of tall towers so that they can reach the wind. A wind turbine's blades are joined to a short stick called a drive shaft. When the wind turns the blades, they turn the drive shaft. The turning drive shaft moves gears. These gears turn the generator, which spins magnets around wires. This makes electricity.

This is a horizontal wind turbine. These common turbines generally have two or three blades.

Farms That Capture Wind

A wind farm sounds like a place to grow wind. In fact, wind farms are places that change wind into electricity. Wind farms sometimes use hundreds of wind turbines.

Wind farm turbines are big. The largest turbines have blades that are longer than a football field! A midsized turbine has blades that are 135 feet (40 m) long. Its tower is 260 feet (79 m) tall. The Snyder Wind Project, in western Texas, has even taller turbines. Together with their towers, these turbines are taller than the Statue of Liberty. This wind farm's 421 turbines provide electricity for 220,000 houses.

This wind farm is in Yucca Valley, California. Wind farms are an important energy source in California.

Where Are the Wind Farms?

There are big wind farms in Texas, California, Iowa, Tennessee, and many other states. Delaware is even building a wind farm in the ocean, 6 miles (10 km) off the coast! What do these places have in common? They are all windy.

Engineers study the wind and give a wind code to each area. In the United States, the least windy places earn a one rating. The windiest places get a seven. Wind farms will work only in areas that have at least a three rating. These places tend to be in the middle of prairies or on mountains. They can also be off the coasts in the ocean.

This offshore wind farm is in Denmark. When its turbines need to be fixed, workers reach them by helicopter!

Many places do not have strong winds. However, smaller turbines can work fine there. Small turbines need less wind to work than large turbines. Some small wind turbines have blades that are only 9 feet (3 m) across. Farmers use these turbines to pump water for animals. Slightly bigger turbines make electricity for individual houses or farms.

Other than their size, small turbines usually look just like large turbines. However, engineers are trying new **designs**, too. One design even looks like a coiled spring! These new designs may be able to make electricity from even lighter wind.

A single turbine can supply most, or even all, of the energy needed to run a farm like this one.

When the wind blows, turbines make clean electricity. However, if the wind does not blow, there is no electricity. Electricity generated by wind power cannot be stored easily. It must be moved to where it will be used. It is hard to move electricity over long distances. Since people do not often live in the windiest areas, engineers must find ways to connect turbines and cities.

The wind must also blow steadily for wind power to be successful. If the wind is really strong one day and weak the next, turbines will not work well. Finally, some people think turbines are ugly and ruin beautiful scenery.

Electricity may travel hundreds of miles (km) between wind farms and people who use it to power things like hair driers.

19

Wind power was once fairly expensive, but now the cost of it has been going down. Generating electricity using wind power now costs just a little more than making electricity from coal. However, wind power creates none of the pollution that using coal does. Also, while fossil fuels, such as coal, are running out, wind power is renewable.

Today, many more people are buying wind turbines. Some people are buying small turbines to put on a home or farm. Big companies are buying large turbines and setting up wind farms. As wind turbines get better, we may find that some of our energy problems are blown away!

Wind energy is becoming more common. In 2008, about 4,000 wind turbines were put up in the United States.

Wind Energy Timeline

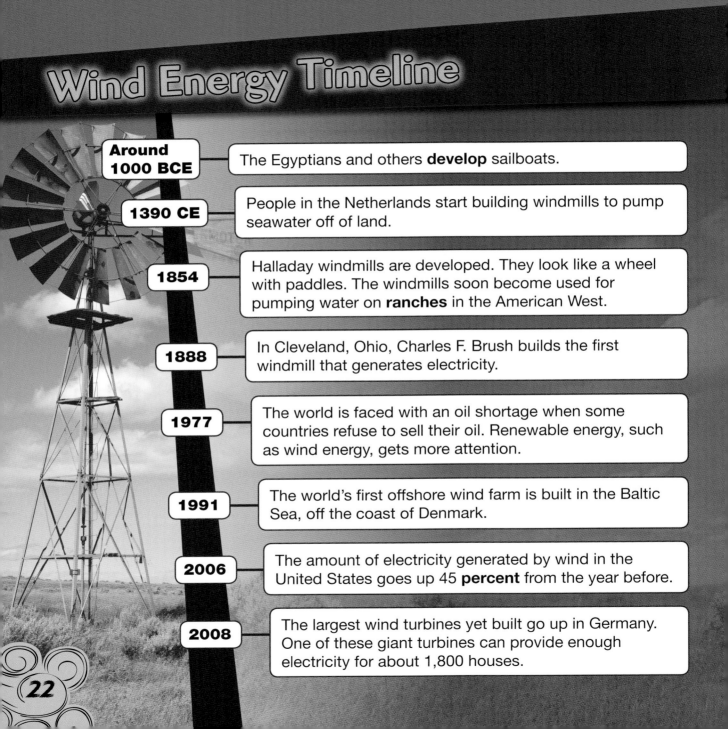

Around 1000 BCE — The Egyptians and others **develop** sailboats.

1390 CE — People in the Netherlands start building windmills to pump seawater off of land.

1854 — Halladay windmills are developed. They look like a wheel with paddles. The windmills soon become used for pumping water on **ranches** in the American West.

1888 — In Cleveland, Ohio, Charles F. Brush builds the first windmill that generates electricity.

1977 — The world is faced with an oil shortage when some countries refuse to sell their oil. Renewable energy, such as wind energy, gets more attention.

1991 — The world's first offshore wind farm is built in the Baltic Sea, off the coast of Denmark.

2006 — The amount of electricity generated by wind in the United States goes up 45 **percent** from the year before.

2008 — The largest wind turbines yet built go up in Germany. One of these giant turbines can provide enough electricity for about 1,800 houses.

Glossary

blades (BLAYDZ) The wide, flat parts of something.

coils (KOYLZ) The rings or curls of things that are wound up.

designs (dih-ZYNZ) The plans or the forms of things.

develop (dih-VEH-lup) To work out or form.

engineers (en-juh-NEERZ) Masters at planning and building engines, machines, roads, and bridges.

fossil fuels (FO-sul FYOOLZ) Fuels, such as coal, natural gas, or gasoline, that were made from plants that died millions of years ago.

generate (JEH-neh-rayt) To make.

grind (GRYND) To crush into tiny pieces.

millstones (MIL-stohnz) Heavy, circular stones used for making grain into a powder.

percent (pur-SENT) One part of 100.

pumps (PUMPS) Things that remove liquid from one place and move it to another.

ranches (RAN-chiz) Large farms for raising cattle, horses, or sheep.

source (SORS) The place where something starts.

turbines (TER-bynz) Motors that turn by a flow of water or air.

Index

A
air, 4, 6

B
blades, 8, 10, 12

C
coils, 10

D
designs, 16

E
Egyptians, 8, 22
electricity, 4, 10, 12, 16, 18, 20, 22
engineers, 14, 16, 18

F
fossil fuels, 4, 20

L
lakes, 4

M
magnets, 10
millstones, 8

N
Nile River, 8

P
pollution, 4, 20
power, 4, 18, 20
pumps, 8

R
ranches, 22

S
sailboats, 4, 6, 22
smoke, 4
source, 4

T
turbines, 4, 6, 10, 12, 16, 18, 20, 22

U
United States, 4, 14, 22

W
wheat, 8

Web Sites

Due to the changing nature of Internet links, PowerKids Press has developed an online list of Web sites related to the subject of this book. This site is updated regularly. Please use this link to access the list:
www.powerkidslinks.com/pow/wind/